Illusion of an Overwhelm

John Amen

ALSO BY John Amen

POETRY
Christening the Dancer (2003)
More of Me Disappears (2005)
At the Threshold of Alchemy (2009)
strange theater (2015)

COLLABORATIVE
The New Arcana (with Daniel Y. Harris, 2012)

MUSIC
All I'll Never Need (2004)
Ridiculous Empire (2008)

Illusion of an Overwhelm

Illusion of an Overwhelm

John Amen

NYQ Books™

The New York Quarterly Foundation, Inc.
New York, New York

NYQ Books™ is an imprint of
The New York Quarterly Foundation, Inc.

The New York Quarterly Foundation, Inc.
PO Box 2015 Old Chelsea Station
New York, NY 10113

www.nyq.org

First Edition

Set in Adobe Garamond and Garage Gothic

Layout and Design: Thia Powers

Cover Art: "Can You See Me Now?" © 2017 Thia Powers

Author Photo: Chad Weeden

Library of Congress Control Number: 2017936068

ISBN: 978-1-63045-048-9

I was a letter, I was a grape of verse,
I was a book you dream before you write.
  Osip Mandelstam

Take me to you, imprison me, for I,
Except you enthrall me, never shall be free,
Nor ever chaste, except you ravish me.
  John Donne

Who knows but that, on the lower frequencies,
I speak for you?
  Ralph Ellison

Love leads me on, from thought to thought,
from mountain to mountain, since every path blazed
proves opposed to the tranquil life.
  Petrarch

and when we speak we are afraid
our words will not be heard
nor welcomed
but when we are silent
we are still afraid
So it is better to speak
remembering
we were never meant to survive
  Audre Lorde

Contents

Hallelujah Anima

*And is sin not
a tunnel to God?*
—Anonymous

1

The purpose of desire
is to propagate desire
& its concomitant recoil:
ambivalence is truth.

Anima works the cattle prod, works the courtiers,
a new breed texting resentment poems
to the hum of an electric choker.

I chased Anima before I even met her,
black clouds gathering over the water,
still chase her through labyrinths of ache,
pining for that tropical season
when I was heir to a lovesick tune
in these more temperate times
I no longer hear.

A man drags his secrets from dream to dream,
secrets that drag him through a hundred skins.
Anima says *give them to me*,
but she never takes them,
& I can't just let them go.

2

From a basement of sleep, I hear your footsteps on the roof &
bound those endless stairs three at a time toward waking. I can
save you from yourself, I think. Then it's me alone on the edge
of the roof beneath the satellites, mouthing an apology, & I hear
you on the street, laughing with strangers—*do it, do it,* you say
over & over—calling me into the darkness.

3

I was never a better dancer than when my tongue darted across
your thigh, gauze curtains fluttering in a holocaust wind. Other
refugees waited in other rooms. I'm sure there was glass on the
floor, probably an overturned easel. The woman with the blue hat
shuffled a tarot deck. Something meaty was burning in the oven.
August, it was always August. Birds kept slamming into the
windowpanes. I recall neighbors screaming outside, someone
banging on the door, smoke rising through the floorboards.

4

after Amerika

We rode in a tank called Ambition. You hollered into the backseat, your lips weren't moving, what I smelled was defeat playing on the radio. I wish you could've seen the circus in my body, longing with its acrobatics. I swung forward to light your cigarette, slipping from the wire, living & living to tell our story. Then flames flashed blue to yellow, our words in the waiting room, the prognosis that lingered at dusk, a world plunging into its coma. Thirty-eight days in a sun-flooded room, painting still-lifes & self-portraits, at night combing the sky for mercy. We didn't believe in curfews or roll calls, we never surrendered to the countdown.

5

after TA

Every night I lose my ring & license in department stores &
amusement parks, digging for a queen in derelict hives, scoping
out safe houses & bordellos, my moods streak & swing, rotating
like stock images on a website. I crash in diners, art houses, &
crumbling cinemas, fall into line as if applying for a day-job,
another pig frozen in a hotel bar, burdened by a story he carries
but can't manage to sing. Anima chews her boredom, flirting with
the clerks, eyeing a soldier willing to go AWOL. I'm in charge of
her jazz guillotine, the subs have been assembling it for years.

6

after JK

I wake, your side of the bed's empty.
I can't recall what's been resolved,
what still teeters like a wineglass
balanced on the edge of a table.

I rummage through negatives,
shadows of you I met in passing.
A breeze writhes in the curtain,
the wildfire across the valley lunges but never leaps.
I'm receiving postcards twice a month
from a man with the same name
as our son who died in the war.

I imagine that you stir minutes later,
you wonder if you fell asleep on a train
& missed your stop, spinning to see me,
or not, as I saw you, or didn't,
how we pass each other in a corridor,
blind with searching, mumbling in the quiet,
what's next? what's next? what's next?

7

I clatter down West Capital at 10:56,
shovel rattling in the truck bed,
Anima under the tarp whispering the Lord's prayer.
I sing along with the voice on the radio,
tune so blue it can't be dated,
horns parting the fog.

I don't hand-wring about what's to come,
instructions are provided.
I go where I go, the dead go where they go;
the others, supposedly quick,
fill their mouths & tamp their envy;
gospels in the flesh, glowing or not,
point me homeward.

I vow to love forever, but it's nature's joke
that wayward lives contract & vanish,
the desirous lose their faith & forget,
death keeps sprouting from conscience & marrow.
I'm trying to purge the frequencies,
stash these tears & faces, these final confessions,
I have permission to throw the first stone.

8

What happened to Jul with the blond hair & brown eyes? Rachael who used to turn & wink at me as she belted her moody tunes, swimming in those minor keys? We've been through three singers in six months. I'm leaving one execution to attend another. I need to learn a different way of breathing. I need to learn a different tuning. Anima calls to me from beyond the smog, beyond my solo. I float past the soup lines & overflowing clinics, out past the city limits where new towers are already being built & hammers blaze 24/7. Anima waits like an exotic scale, like an improvisation I've yet to claim. I'm unmooring from the world I wanted to love, leaving behind its sharp edges, its legalistic memory.

9

a la M

In the heyday of fuck-sense & Ecstasy,
blood spiked under your skin,
our own big bang, soon a green universe
of debt & desire expanding & shrinking,
our lives a contract we never signed.

I bargain with a salesman,
saying *I won't be a servant*,
the salesman riffing *who do you think you serve?*
I have to admit *I serve myself.*
Someone pumps a car horn, I turn my head,
I'm shouting your name into a cellphone,
condos & gas stations as far as I can see.

You appear with apples & cheese,
hors d'oeuvres I devour all the way to the suburbs,
arguing with a tv, breaking the key in the lock.
So many dress rehearsals,
I realize I don't recognize your voice,
you're speaking in, perhaps always spoke in,
a language I never learned.

10

for T 4

You wince & wander, succumb & evade, savoring regret as sweet as summer melon. Desire's what you desire, not the repast, not fulfillment. You think you chase satiety, instead driven deeper into cravings that circle themselves. This is your myth of origin, how your precious exile began—this is the way you convince yourself you don't belong, so you don't.

11

Anima packs her bag on Sunday,
buckets of black paint slosh over my bed,
my desk, the usual list of curios.
Later I carry a blank page down the hall
of a public library. The security guard
places it on a shelf, hands me a lottery ticket.
Each night the jackpot swells, each
night I swear off another word.

I forget the clues & equations
that need to be discussed,
a minotaur with the voice of a diva
waits in the car, waits in the stars.
Years sober & I'm still doping my shadow,
chasing a siren through the alleys.

The sham I see in the world
is the sham I see in myself,
the matrix that never ended a war.
No one ever blew down the door of want
& came to singing in a choir.
Some say there's no such thing as rehearsal,
I say that's all there is.

12

for Hank's Group

In another life,
I'm not the boy in the chicken coop,
whose wagon lost a wheel between peaks,
who couldn't keep the tune when it mattered,
I'm the giant who spends his day
repairing elegant instruments,
sending his instructions by messenger
to all the cities that count.

I've learned,
what's an apocalypse while it looms
can be a light rain when it arrives.
I've mastered being in several places at once,
how to answer to multiple names.
I fly into buildings,
crashing into the ocean below.
Over & over I comb the depths,
trying to find the body,
my body,
I do this while
wringing my hands in the chicken coop.

The fry-bell's sounding,
the damsel in the cotton field is singing again.
I have to remember
not to be seduced by a single narrative,
that her song's one of a thousand narratives,
a stolen gun hidden beneath a mound of leaves.
Already there's a cold edge in the air,
I hear the hounds barking in the distance,
the sun's rising or setting, depending on your view.
You could say *it looks like curtains.*
You could say *we're finally getting started.*

13

Anima's script calls for me to play the jaded maestro thrashing a
piano for change. I wander the warehouse, stepping over mangled
scales, swatches, mannequins, Anima yelling *cut*. I'm the keeper
of slugs. I have a private cell. I wear jazz chords like businessmen
wear ties. I can't stop babbling about love. I need someone to tune
the piano before I set it on fire. Hallelujah Anima, my illusion
keeps giving keeps taking.

14

A black moccasin coils in the roots.
We need to step across the stones before high tide.
I tell you *we can make it.*
You reply *we can't make it.*

Years later at the carnival,
we meet behind the abandoned paper plant
where the mud never dries,
near the lock where my father drowned,
waving his compass & burning map,
where your mother disappeared,
clutching her pride & fake pearls.
We dismantle the story
over shine-berries & hindsight gospel.
I keep a gold shovel to un-dig the details.
You post *I'm sorry we couldn't make it.*

Don't worry about the black moccasin,
don't worry about the fire screaming across the water.
Forget the wild animals behind us,
so many wild animals I can't remember.

There's a direct line from our flailing
to a house we've never seen but will surely recall,
we'll know each other, we'll find the ladders in the storm,
everything we need to move forward.

15

Anima slumps in the corner, speechless, a fixture I inherited.
If you're silent long enough, people invent stories, they
mythologize your silence: Anima, the silent oracle. When the
world stops groping, when photographers & journalists speed
off in their vans, I belt Anima's arm, plunge the plunger, her
dead, dark eyes scanning me as if I were a petroglyph. I remove
her gowns & prostheses, I wipe her pits & genitals. *Watch*, I
threaten, *I'll pack my earplugs & blindfold, I'll leave you*, truth is
I've left a dozen times, I never leave—the courtier, assassin,
caregiver, I'm everything I was trained to be.

16

In mid-June, a day arrives & departs
like a song without a bridge,
& all the world's a limbo of bulldozers & debt.

I'm not Odysseus or Iago, rather
a prime number running his errands, shuffling
through the strip mall, through bloom & wither,
which is to say my souvenirs remind me
I don't actually exist.

Desire?—desire's the gate in the backyard
swinging to the Disney simulacrum of paradise
that detonates every sunset, leaving a pile of wreckage
where I stand & wait for the spaceship
to rain coins emblazoned with my image.

Anima sits naked in the brown lawn, smirking.
Most of my life is distraction.

PS

for 3

There's a woman
who stands at the end of my street,
who carries in her purse
a small package with my address on it.
The persistent fear is that everything you know
is made of fog. *It is*, she mouths from the end of the street.
The audience is about to begin laughing.

If there's one talent I have
it's an ability to convince myself I'm on a winning streak
while waiting for the next load of dirt to land,
ringing a bell in the darkness
after the grievers have gone.

It's my drug of choice,
chasing the headline that gives evaporating returns.
I'd kill Jesus for a bullhorn,
but I'm not the only one fighting for leftovers.
Footsteps in the leaves,
louder & louder to the next county,
heels cracking all the way
to another lifetime.

Grace

for Stefan

In the beginning, a little blind spot,
o little big bang, little blind spot
becomes the universe, gives gravity a job,
keeps you clutching your hand grenade,
fingers twitching on the lever—
ok to think but not to throw ok to think but not to throw
Remind yourself: it's 2017, don't let 1971
detonate in your lap, take out the living room,
the house, the dream it's taken decades to find,
years lost in the swamp & fire.

I'm not the first to experience
effort as little more than a bunker
to hide in while inconsequence,
with its platoon of dead-ends & sabotages,
marches its way, a monsoon
rearranges the furniture, indifference
cranks up the volume on the radio.

I don't like writing my own obituary
while across town another part of me is christened;
still, I wear *brother you better believe*
none of this is going to work out
like a suit of armor, like a drip IV.
Like bulletproof wings I flap to find
someone else already signed the contracts, delivered the mail,
threw his body between the exploding grenade

& the rest of the world. My years
have been punctuated by small salvations
I can never explain, they arrive like sleep or waking,
like going home the morning after the bunker's lost,
always the morning after.

The American Myths

1

for R

J scales a ladder up & up a steep pitch of memory
toward a smallish star, writhing from the manhole,
black son clawing through black film, his black eyes
rolling across a patio as the guests applaud, sloshing
their olives & gin. Dr. Kilgus hacks the London broil.
After a group charade involving a breast pump & a

petri dish, J's mother's bound to the scaffold, his
father sparks the Jacksons tucked beneath the tinder.
J wails in a red world, witnesses the gluttony of fire,
sensation as a second birth & first demise: root of
ambivalence. A wet nurse in camouflage delivers
the needle. J's scaled & weighed, paperwork's filed,

he's swaddled in steel wool, wrapped in cellophane,
carted to an empty barracks on the outskirts of town.
Someone croons the national anthem through a static
intercom. Someone stages an aptitude test. J finds
his feet, his hands, unzips his innocence like a clown
shedding a costume. He steps forth a full-grown man.

2

Inconsolable J, bluer than a harp at dusk,
weens himself a homeless beast, exiled from
the mothership of dirt & sky. O white God,
aid him, crack his bedrock memory, he studies
the nightmare but not its source, perplexed
by envy & vertigo. He cruises the grocery,

mast-bound, palms pressed to ears, scuttled
in the booze aisle beside the fortified wines.
Fire's a lorelei, & he's star-struck when it
comes to cash, the cold diva, he can't wise up,
can't shake her wiles. O white God, in self-
forgetting all that remains for a man is vanity.

Shatter J's trance, give him back his early eyes,
music without private rooms, unearth his first
face buried beneath a mudslide of serial faces,
that trickster in the glass, his habit of knowing.
Drown his illusions, o white God, ∞ choked
by a name. O white God, is there a real world?

3

J slurps a diet soda, checking his texts outside
El Paraíso on date night. His wife enters, heels
& orange scarf, witchy in a sable blouse. See
his slang & emoticons blaze, the hootenanny
in his roadhouse groin, how he closes the door
he opens, such is ambivalence. Such is PTSD.

He haggles over refills, the number of shrimp
in his paella. Frustration's his oldest pal, though
every meal he raises his glass to *flow!*, each
morning a bump & pop to his first port of call.
Forgetting's his only trick, the one he's honed,
wings that dissolve without warning. He belches,

regretting his appetite, reflux a familiar dessert.
J revved on coffee, pays the bill, tips the valet,
his .32 whispering from the glove compartment.
Home, he dry swallows three Ambiens, revises
his will & health-care docs, wakes in a flowerbed
unto the white father. When J prays, he plunges.

4

I know the part, hobbling to the white bathroom
at three AM, clench & release, the bloody enamel,
my white father & his Super PAC cronies nodding
in the observation deck. Dr. Kilgus whets his blade.
Cheers & applause. Tweets & reviews. The click
of the camera. I play the moody artiste. Later I play

solitaire as the cellphone rings. Later I send a text,
my dear white father's top ten hypocrisies, no one
dares to respond. I pose in the backyard, selfie in
Union blue, dropping a pin for the missing link,
who miscarried in the wings, my mother who died
strapped to a plastic rood, burned during rush hour.

I throw my fav rock at a stranger, who throws her
fav rock at me, all for a love that failed to gestate,
floating in three inches of red water. I solve riddles
& research WWII. I change my gauze, still insisting,
I'm a full citizen, though I'm really just a black son,
enraged when no one answers my unspoken prayers.

5

for CW

I perch when night rises, black hours
stretch like the dead mother's white legs.
It's my turn to breathe, house in a coma,
the black son locked in the ham house,
Dr. Kilgus snoring in his mezzanine
as I uncoil my dread on carpeted floor,

examining its fangs by television light,
the glow of cable noir. The fixer, arsonist,
saboteur, by day how they riot, now
retreat & doze to cricket song. I recall
you don't need accountability to live a
😃 life, be saved by love or curiosity.

The game seems winnable when I'm alone,
the hundred filibusters trailing into silence,
each vagary a direct line to the empire.
Grease & sugar are the gateways to God,
but solitude's the cosmic nipple. I'm numb
to the wheel, numb to my dear white dad.

6

The after party's a dress rehearsal,
an off-off-Broadway retread. I skulk
in a dim foyer, scanning for Amanda,
we knew each other in our 53rd St days.
Arthur's already out of body, eyes spin
like red pennies, his alter ego waking

from a corporate dream. Dr. Kilgus
saws the turkey, pink juice squirting
on a yellow tablecloth, a dozen photos
of the dead *familia* propped on the mantel.
Libby sports her necklace of a lost son,
black as an ash pond. She quotes Plato

while flirting with the resident killer.
Lu swills poison on demand. We're all
critics, & the night's a bomb, impatience
trussed in foil, gaffes echoing in sound-
proofed Tupperware. We lift our aerosols,
toast the white God, beast of America.

7

for CN

Woods are for sale, perfect for a parking lot,
owners will throw in antique sculpture of the
mother strapped to a flowery rood, hologram
of navy-blue flames requiring no maintenance.
Locale zoned for political correctness, includes
shrine erected in 2008 in honor of the lost boy,

how he bit the nipple, watched as his white father
tossed Jacksons, huffing the bellows of gossip,
his mother's reddening flesh. Years he'd fan
the pyre, gorge on ash, roll in it, he'd become
the black son, spend his teens & twenties in exile,
rising finally as the hustler of his generation.

Now's his chance to sway public opinion, white
God as his personal Super PAC. The black son
thumbs-up for the camera, toothy on the billboard.
The black son roaring on Super Bowl Sunday.
This is how he storms the world; that's payback,
baby, manifest destiny, that's o bless America.

8

Cleveland/Philadelphia

The wrath of the white God is systemic,
a secret ingredient in your dead mother's
blood casserole. Envy's the resident
ghost in your seed, what shoves a plot
toward its crisis. Beauty too is a vampire,
& don't forget: no victory without hubris.

Grays gather at a local diner, Blues in a
fast-food lobby, zealot & apostate alike
clawing at the white God, another filibuster
beside a smoking pyre, the white-legged
mother fading behind the menstrual curtain
in the hands of a white father postpartum,

their black son gumming a French fry.
Nine months in the dead mother's womb,
decades under the white father's tongue—
dread's a crowbar wedged between your ribs
neither Prozac nor Ambien can dissolve.
With each breath, you feel the crack of bone.

9

for SL

Twenty-six years sober, I smell vodka in the tulips,
aged bourbon in the blankets, water reeks of gin.
Twenty-six years, still hear my dead mother calling,
drunk in the hammock, drooling into her cleavage.
She slurs *help me* while guzzling her Chardonnay.
I see the white father in me, I hear his *no*, the way

he lowered his magnifying glass on every prayer,
our petitions curling to smoke, he planted dread
in my belly, a C-section / implant after I passed out
in the ice shed. I'd wake in the driveway, gutted.
Now I light the rood as he lit the rood. *No, I can't,*
I respond, though I could, my dead mother in flames,

my show & tell: an iron, rusted nails, loaded dice,
jujus found in the weedy backyard. Fast-forward:
my wife spread-eagled in a shadowbox. I curse my
white father's shimmering crown, a black son vowing
to return home & avenge the women of his dreams.
They call me *liar*, you watch I'll prove them wrong.

10

after Bigger

J'll def prevail, he has before, his dead mother
pleading on the rood, the asp in his gut, he begs
his white father for a loan. It's bad on the west side,
parking lots & yards bloated with litter, swinging
nooses, but a home's not all mulch & manicure,
& a white father's a bank with a bottomless mouth.

J can't protect what's untrammeled in the world,
can't feel the divine hanging a sec from his skin,
begins to bargain as the verdict's read. Each gunner
in the firing line's his brother, he crumples with ♥
gushing in his black blood— ♥ the white father,
♥ the dead mother, game money, & still he has a

knack for leaving when he needs himself the most.
That's trifling. True, J sails in circles as often as lines,
but his wins are exotic ports that can't be docked
without him. Hours founder as he drags the straits
of adrenaline & cortisol. Luck's his compass, maybe
his only compass, again he eddies toward open sea.

11

Act 1, J enters a billion miles from the sun, gales
raging across a suburban landscape, clouds heavy
with dry ash & vortices; ice clutches the awnings,
encasing the strip mall. Act 2, J stretches & shrugs
off his pharmaceutical haze: like white father, like
black son. Here the vets & hurricane angels dwell,

wringing shelter in the dumpsters, each afternoon
talk-talk & methadone, how the script turns in light
of a burning Jackson. Act 3, Kilgus licks the blade.
Act 4, in the absence of awe, the white father appears
with a rulebook, game money, the dead mother sings,
Scale my legs, o son come home, my womb's a-waiting.

J's iliad: combing the empty womb for a wife.
J's odyssey: combing the empty womb for a wife.
Act 5, a spaceship hovers above the bank, alien speck
bobbing in the white father's breath. A rope's lowered.
Grab it, the prop master bellows, but J's off script,
black son on a bare stage, middle finger to the sky.

12

*An electrical insect control system's erected in the
center of the labyrinth. White father gnaws a bone,
dead mother breastfeeds her black doll beneath a
plastic rood.* Action. White father & I spew stories,
trying to outdo each other. I riff on my Navy days.
Zap. He opens with his timeless hit, the couple ousted

from a gated community for picnicking on the grass.
Zap. I unravel my years of addiction, how I poured
& plunged, ate pills by the vial, lived in a rusty cage
with a ghost & a mourning dove, finally coming down
in a Brooklyn intensive care unit. Zap. He ripostes
with his standby re the infamous deluge. *A group of*

homeless men forms. Zap. I close with my tearjerker,
ma & pa waving in the driveway as I fled Topeka.
Zap. The homeless men award me the paper crown.
We piss in unison as the white father grinds his teeth,
retreating into darkness. We crucify the dead mother,
dismember the black doll. *Smoke, mock-waving.* Zap.

13

J in the kitchen of his scrapbook home, Etch-
a-Sketches strewn on a marble floor, a dead
mother rehearsing voodoo, running spells while
dicing a yellow onion. The white father fumes
in his office, perusing stats & odds, polishing
his good-luck rood. He lives on cough drops,

stashing his payoffs in a Super PAC, he rages
on Christmas, at the mention of anything Greek.
The DA buries his crimes, a dismissal each time
the op-eds subside. J hocks what he can steal,
sucking a glass pipe, a mason jar of Aristocrat.
He badmouths his white father's newest how-to,

a penny dreadful of insider etiquette, installation
funded by America, Inc. Headlines fall from J's
brow, piling by his bedroom door, his vocabulary
stashed in his dead mother's throat. We all know
a white brother carries the world on his back, but
a black son—a black son carries hell in his heart.

14

for Philip

I'm the black son; doesn't matter if this is factual,
it's my life story, the metaphor that locks my throat.
Raised in a flooded town, I belly-crawled dirt roads
in a county of Stars & Bars, pale Jesus & pit bulls,
succubi lying open-legged in a hayloft. My eleventh
birthday, I grabbed the rattler from the priest, held

its face to my face. I watched its eyes turn to glass
as the congregation booed. Don't believe the white
father, his myth of origin; truth is, he turns a crank
in the background, he keeps the keys, he sprays the
fig tree with pesticide when believers aren't looking.
Don't entertain that crap about the dead mother being

sculpted from a rib, bear in mind that this white father
is simply another white father in a line of white fathers,
each of whom burned in a pyre of Jacksons, screwed
by his own ballyhoo. That said, there are indeed doors
in the white father's house that can only be opened
by a black son. Not every black son. This black son.

15

In white America, every word flies in two directions, we
use Jacksons to split a black son, bury you in the numbers,
& when the white father prods you from his house, as surely
he will, you vanish without looking back, you spend years

on a scaffold—IRAs, 401Ks, insurance, a world of
pyramids & smoke, prescriptions & proscriptions that might

win you admission to a grand gala that fizzled decades ago.
The white father packages his rules, envy lubes this world,
sells you to close the gap, a lure of cash & trophies, instead
stirs another brand of missing. Scripture says: *every white
father must a black son kill.* Conventional wisdom counters:
every black son must a white father bless, revising the books

when it comes to love. A black son strives to keep a home,
pipes rupture, roof & floors collapse. Fixtures spark & death-
rattle, appliances seize, the lawn's a backstabber. It's torture
to study a Beatrice, not that you crave what you see, rather:
you see nothing at all. Give up your keys & swinging doors:
the bed you crash by night, maybe by morning you remain.

16

A camera's wedged between a black son's thoughts,
lodged in his labored breath. Each inhale, he hears
a mechanical whir, colleagues laugh when he forgets
his lines. His dead mother's his prompter, whispering
in the wings, shaving her legs in an empty tub while
perusing a redacted holy ordinance, blood streaking

the enamel. Hullabaloo & much ado. Repeat. Later
she lies drunk on the living room floor, surrounded
by utensils, shattered Ming vases, a bank statement.
When the black son clenches his eyes, he beholds his
dead mother in anime, her lurid lap dance. He tucks a
Jackson in her G-string. He's the uncredited blackface,

lip-synching a Jim Crow plucked from the blind pigs
of America. His white father owns a chain of planets
severed from the sun. His dead mother retreats to her
iron maiden. A black son smokes an IOU to the ink,
he smokes it for all it's worth, hacking under a globe
of debt—his own or someone else's—that's his forte.

17

My white father proposes to my dead mother, fireflies
pulsing in the smog. As resident black son, I carry my
logic on my back, heir to the rood, scattering Jacksons
among the homeless at the strip mall. I'm the exemplary
cavalier, *yes mam, no mam*, the keeper of the calendar,
trolling for razors & potted meat at the warehouse club.

My white father's incidental without me; yeah, for now,
he snuffs me every red Tuesday over eggs & headlines,
but soon, some blue Friday, I'll eclipse him, freeze him
with his own spell, steal back my breath, unloose a golem
in his milk-&-ivory mansion. Meanwhile I broker a peace
between the delegates, all white & dead, each hoping I'll

assume the family business, days filled with foreclosures,
flipping properties, steering the Super PAC. My parents
aren't married yet, I haven't been born yet. They have no
idea I'm the ring bearer, riding a mutant gene toward their
radio voices. A black son's story is the same before flesh
as during flesh: the love he demands is the love he rejects.

18

If a black son refuses to be a black son, even then
he's a black son, fumbling in the smog, runs errands
while shouldering a rood—grocery, gas, Americano,
duct tape. His dead mother's thighs crush his rib cage,
she presses her mouth to his mouth, nails shredding his
black skin. He has miles to sing before the dream ends,

before his dead mother becomes his wife, he mustn't
be distracted. His white father rages over the buffet,
my stupid black son, spilling red sauce on his bow tie.
A black son sleeps through his alarm, crawls from bed
an hour late—vacuum, brunch, porno for the paralyzed.
He needs a dead mother like thunder needs a shotgun,

needs a white father like a dinosaur needs a meteorite.
He's the straw boss gorging on donuts, shaking hands
in the long white hallway, gagging on his dead mother,
his white father, pockets thick with undeclared Jacksons.
Creditors stalk him at the strip mall, his red Gethsemane,
the taxman ties on a bib, the way a real killer can wait.

My Gallery Days

1

for Louisa

A purple hearse idled beside a green ladder:
      Bill Casaman's Tompkins Pk funeral.
He nailed his brain on webcam: lo-fi suicide.

We recall his Gotham talks while staggering
through the dog run, cheeks smeared w/ fake blood,
      confetti wafting from the Christodora.

You were right of course:
      resistance is a midwife w/ a bad attitude.
Vanity however remained our forceps,
      how we could milk the situation.

Bloggers emerged: *Casaman, disappearing ink
on the devil's palm.* I counter-posted: *Ambivalence
      is our common denominator.* For 3 days,

his memento mori flapping on the gallery door.

2

for Donovan

You arrived circa New Year's, Apollo of the East Side,
          posturing in vintage fur & pensive on 79th,
     w/in weeks rawboned, a wannabe Artaud
replete w/ nose ring & track marks on pallid skin,
     swarmed by crabs in Washington Heights.

I never dissed yr 1-strokes, how you kneeled for the realists,
but had to spill blood when you puddled (flatlining or not)
          on Vicki's god-clean floor.

          You left behind a duffel bag of stationery
& half-hearted motel sketches, a webpage w/ shattered links.
     Yeah, I ferried you upriver, back to yr momma's blue
blue hospital, could've been worse than 30 days on a gurney.

          But let's be generous:
no one'll forget yr impromptu sonnets @ Bleecker & dawn.

3

for RJ

Five o'clock—prime time for boots & the Wild West,
             yr opening line though I can't say
I heard what came next, Helen's 3-legged Cerberus
       yapping on 33rd   the racket of the Alphabet.

      Then the interminable open mic,
      3 crossdressers heaving a fridge
out the 2nd-story window (to a stillborn villanelle).

Yr co-feature bombarded w/ minutia, a robot reciting
diary entries from a typical day in the word factory.
You blurted *I wish I'd taken that desk job @ the bank.*
Wtf would you do w/ vacation time in the Hamptons?

      Take this as a compliment, you're 0 if not adept
@ advancing yrself, I mean that to eulogize yr pitch-
perfect karma, so why da hangdog face? Why da huff?

4

for L & "the 4th shift"

The earnest & untrodden turn the worst of cynics,
      an artist & her sandbox by funding parted.

Ours is the *real* lost generation, days like vanishing data,
      insomniac Superflats inclined to brood,
can a nihilist find her voice in the khaki suburbs?

Railbirds gathered stones then da stoning over potluck.

      Shalom the aesthetes w/ bowlers,
Peirrot w/ his switchblade & *Complete Poems of Jurgan.*
      Shalom our fluorescent hub,
      who wants to flagellate our resident naïf?
      —hooked on soda, cough syrup, & energy bars,
      nodding beside his iPad on a polyester leash.

You pawned our sketches to Mr. Pharm, who attended
the opening, a final Rx hoopla to hang my gloat on.

5

for Sydney Blanket

—who drawled *I'm the maestro of this carnival,*
posing with pastel bouquet & acct books @ dawn.

An hour in yr office, I was asthmatic for a week.

Diva, damsel, or Scaramouche in drag,
you were seamless w/ a script—wooing the outsiders,
entrancing a gatekeeper,
lecturing the snoutplowers of this crumpled city,

every week those video blasts,
the elegy for Evie, who found silence but never returned.

You posed in garters for a masthead,
wrapped yrself nude in the Biltmore rug, the blank
checks rolled all the way to a taxman w/ a red guillotine.

I applaud you, particularly yr crescendos,
skipping indie world straight to a wall @ the MOMA.

6

for Leslie

Yr mural never dried, the courts couldn't corral
the do-gooders w/ their spraypaint & scripture.

To hoard acrylics in a shrinking room,
  counting pills while yr cellphone bleats:
    "por. of a saboteur as a y. doormat."

Bloggers trampled the broadband,
  you swilled a month of vitriol,
    a semester in retrograde, untenured.

Interpretation so often exceeds intention,
  why's it always the waif
    who's accused of being the witch?

You nodded from the Bowery Mission to the news
back to the Bowery Mission w/ a Demerol smoothie
  —treading Augustine 'til no morning after.

7

for Desdemona

We're finally legit ya sd, waving the IRS report
—that summer the galleries overrun by forgers & finks.

(It'd be sensational to release an anthology of memoirs by
        convicted perjurers, a kinda authenticity project)

I voted for yr pitch to film Les Kleptos @ Green Flea,
just didn't want a grant to dilute my circles&squares.

        Gesso was yr signature, bankruptcy macabre,
        all the way to 94th & Mr. Digital's knockoff scam,
        Pollock or was it O'Keeffe in recycled Styrofoam?

        Then ya cartwheel into the Jane Hotel
—ya couldn't say if ya wanted me in fuck or swansong,
        cain't have yr god & devil on the same hobbyhorse.

You're poster 1990s I sd *w/ yr clip & monogrammed needle.*
You replied *I almost love ya when I know you're waiting.*

8

Leslie, I saw yr ghost in the Frederick, those blue
shoes & a Red Bull, yr popularity a summer squall,
debt don't respond to no standard dance moves.

So sorry for polishing off the tortillas,
& I did indeed snag the Benjamins from the mousetrap,
gossiping w/ Laurie over shots.

I added to my resume the 7 credits in Spiegel Park.
Diversion remains the only god I know. Leslie,
could you hear the taxmen & bulldozers in the distance?

In yr finest hour w/ a brush & Bourbon,
oblivious to audits & thunder from Albany,
you choked on the grant & gagged the interview.

A trip to East 9th shifted the mood for an hour,
but damn the coke vapor, a devil kicking in my lungs.

9

I sold "a door closes on east 79th," my father's
HP snuffed beneath a shroud of carbon black,
my childhood faith truncated w/ a single stroke.

I hate this gallery Z sd, tablet in hand.
      I love it I retorted, perfect payback,
            Z w/ his puritanical maxims.

Slime & more slime he typed, a slur on my
favorite minimalist, Ann Dju, I had defended
a week before over animal crackers & a spoon.

Z's swollen blog, the search engines coughed.
Every time Z refreshed, some Midwesterner's
daughter's blood would spatter on a newsfeed.

—that night he turned on me, saying universality
      died w/ Plato. *No* I insisted *it died w/ you.*

10

To the pigs who sang in Hillary's walls.
Stuart trapped between studs, tuneless in the heat,
Carl panting in a doorframe, sick & shaking DTs,
        grunting Provencal love songs
        w/ a Long Island accent.

Ma sanctum sanctorum was desecrated by Photoshop.
Soul collage & music boxes, the vengeful goddess
popped from Hill's mouth, her Gorgon series in yeller.

I removed the tank cover in her half-bath,
        hooked a shriveled man who'd no doubt
drifted for seasons, sworn off his pocket watch
        & eyes as dead as a cold call.

Hill I sd in white *you gotta set the boy free*,
Hill staring in gray, the miles tween Hill & me.

11

Mildred eulogized her stepfather in TX
while I finished her portrait with a palette knife
        during Z's Taurean salon.

I'd never see that kinda doomed again or forget
Mildred wearing long sleeves in muggy Houston.

After the gavel, Mildred's solstice on ECT,
I spent July clean, banged out "The Verdict,"
        a photomontage of Mildred in drag.
I won the ITY grant, the stepfather's daughter
        twitching on a gurney in Somewhere, TX.

3 months later, I was 4 days out of treatment
& already stoned, railing how Mildred slipped away.
        Amidst the racket & regret,
                I skulked past being famous.

12

I'm terror&legerdemain once you peel the persona
I mumbled @ West & Barclay. Ambition's a jealous god,
          mad titan treading the NJ Styx,
     splashing surges crosstown toward Baruch Place.

This changes things sd Louisa, squinting her right eye,
then left, unscrewing the Van Dyke. I cleared my throat,
     came to mid-spike, mid-portrait, & there
was Mississippi Deena, foundering in valium&vodka.

          Corduroy Dennis dropped off 15 irons
& 23 hubcaps, bartered & bantered for shrooms&sugar,
          waving an X-Acto for shrooms&sugar.
Soon it'd be dark, sooner than was bearable, my father's
generation mute, mine fumbling @ the turnstile of narcissism.

O my digital Yahweh, how to capture a grayscale twilight.

13

for I think it was Heather

        April & I studied a green rapture,
free from the gallery for a month w/ pay,
freelancing on the 11th St bronze, commemoration
        of Doggett's last poetic stand:
    already unwired, dissected @ Bethel Main,
    he opened his 8th Ave reading by dropping
his boxer shorts. The 3 Cs: cops, court, commitment.

Jaeger said that Doggett staged the fiasco, it was
his scripted swansong. I never told you a dream I had,
you & Doggett & I were sprawled on the Newburgh pier,
        sharing a calzone, arguing about
Jay Sanford's "unmasked" @ the Brooklyn EuroFest,
when Doggett stood up, dashed a crust to the ripples,
    & proclaimed me the inaugural solipsist!

14

for Nea whose sidekick was Stanislaw

I finally reached Mr. Ed Hauser in Harrisburg,
pitched a grant. *What'sdarush?* ya slurred as if
more important commissions were *indaworks.*

I'd never say *pleaz o nymph grind the gatekeeper,*
        but we coulda used a reed or woody spell
to flank & contain the cannibals of Babel U,
        swarmed in the gallery, filing their teeth.

O, how'd ya justify living with Slaw,
        that drooling tornado?

& 'member Mr. V? *Too much smoke to raise a ghost!*
We were castaways ramming the doors of the MOMA,
        stripping & starving for $$$.
        This is how I think of ya:

Nea, shivering in a doorway, undone by ambition.

15

AM I soared on Adderall, crashing @ dusk,
      Claude on 51st w/ his rainbow pipe,
            dude humming along to Coltrane
standards on tape, dude dead in a snowdrift in May.

      I rode those sirens to Bellevue,
           role-playing w/ a drip-IV
while Dr. Bauman studied his DSM.

      August: the tax scandal @ the co-op,
      bad PR re L's mock auto-da-fé, & no buyers
for my portraits of Heather G, who'd vanished

amidst the pyrotechnics, 4 days cold in a Nyack slum.
      Her obit swept the blogs,
         her face still blows in my sleep,
these spattered rooms I can never leave.

16

I lived like an anchorite on the lee side of kink,
Sigur Rós, Zarathustra, & Kierkegaard's leap,
libido on a binge & o yea Allison's genius grant.

　　　—her all-paid residency in Baltimore,
　　　& me climbing fire escapes on the weekend,
peddling blood to lampoon my family's provincialism.

　　　Accuse her all you like of imitation,
she defended her "Red & Green Docks of Reeding"
　　　all the way to the Whitney in September.

　　　O come on, you remember Allison;
　　　she's ash now on 109th —others did worse,
ventriloquists on forever methadone, their abstracts

sold for change @ yard sales in Bellmore & Syosset,
　　　the years pass like nodding on Coney Island.

17

Overlooking 23rd, Louisa mentioned Mr. Ed Hauser,
contemporary Medici in the Museum of Etiquette.
    Bad information's like a silent migraine
I replied, sloshing my grape juice (transubstantiated)
    on her still dripping canvas.

    Every day you get wispier Louisa argued,
puffing a smoke ring into the room; it rose in the grayscale
& dissipated; like all metaphors, quartered in a moment,
sentenced to a b&w death. *Take this card* she insisted:

Edward Hauser, Department of Conventional Aesthetics

    My lips were chapped, I smelled roadkill.

The gods be loose I sd. *Dis call for basil & a crucifix.*
    Louisa smirked, prodded for a vein in her right arm.

I swear in the silence the music inside me was crumbling.

18

Hijacked by Evie's Dilaudid Rx,
I did my best to illustrate Louisa's limbo,

took me 2 weeks to nail the watery umber
of her Sicilian eyes, mixing & remixing
to invoke that Ophelian aura, flummoxed
by her chosen backdrop (faux "Acanthus" circa 1880).

Grant deadlines converged, I dreamt
I was a tearaway riding south in an empty caboose.
(I wanted to wake beside a steaming river,
pawn my antique palette, I still
wanna talk shop over rare steaks & a blank canvas)

Nothing like a protractor & tube of Windsor red,
Louisa in the doorway wilting & her feet throbbed,
the U of B critics had lambasted her floating studio.

19

for Z

The Am-dream's a 1-stroke I texted *sliced in the dark.*
We're refugees riding a hobbyhorse bareback, art a
bronco bucking its own beat: manifestos are incidental.

Cambret's self-portrait in wire you replied *would be*
perfect in a landfill, choking yr arm with a bungee cord.
You gouged his narrative, the blasts of random subtext,
how type O bubbled from the white mannequin's lips

every 29 seconds (onto a cream carpet): *Fuck his CV,*
replete with emoticons. Jo Reid differed in *The Railbird*:
I'd give my Masterburgs for the rust on Cambret's floor.

You staggered on 14th while palpating yr blog: *Cambret*
& his shooting circle. The York? Best when it was empty.

No s'prise a'tall, during his coronation @ Gallery LG,
ya turn da bootlicker—Cam's Polonius, Brutus, his Iago.

20

for Hillary

Hill: the Salome of tastes, gadfly to abide, posing
w/ tiara & periwinkle works in each hand. Subtitle:
"@ dawn she steals a secret w/out waking the king."

It wasn't trendy to mention Delacroix or Stendhal
'less wooing a gatekeeper in some nonprofit maze.
Well, you did score the Halston: "bondage & ennui:
life in the margins." Thanx for the 60% yeller, sorry
it was July before we noticed yr Bearden was gone.

Still, only a fool would piss *The Canon* for all to see,
improvident to masquerade as the exemplar of a trend.
Bloggers bull-horned, the queen devoured by workers.

You beat the meaning out of color & form, I'll give
you that. *Intention's finally irrelevant* I sd. Hey Hill,
who the fuck nods while perusing grant applications?

21

A forsythia was my burning bush in Williamsburg,
      I then so cavalier barreled into DC.

      (I forgot my notes & sketches)

I knew I'd signed up for a crash w/out the high:
      Louisa, never a bell w/out a bomb.
In short, I joined her asp&gorgon show. We floated
down the Hudson for a nodding day in her doublewide
4 miles from Troy. (w/ skin-board & cheap acrylics)

      I was a surrogate @ best but speared a grant.
      Louisa sd *stay as the jester in residence,*
      I could have the pod & leftover swatches!

(We all have gifts, foresight & diplomacy not hers)

Still, 2 months to brainstorm, & I gained 7 lbs.
Those days everyone was snarling for the limelight.

22

Louisa, wearier than a mime in a straitjacket,
dubbed her self-portrait pointillist, though Z
joked it was connect-the-drool. She couldn't've
cared less about the blogs, nodding to the bank.

I rambled the rooms of the Frederick repeating
only applause & $$$ can balm Louisa's wound!

I don't know what it was about her follow-up—
"the provincial madams"—that wired the devil,
Ed Hauser raging in the dailies & so much vitriol.
In the end, the 9th Circuit had to bang the gavel.

    It's easy to be intimidated by discord,
    I've found that most rebels wanna be liked.

Burying her brushes, a CNA in pressed white,
Louisa hocked her oeuvre to a resident gynecologist.

23

Are all the good curators gone? I sd,
my umpteenth romp in the Frederick,
pausing near Doggett's "paranoid #4,"

that anatomically correct middle finger,
steel & tin, ignored 'til a vandal's rage
blew it primetime, now a logo for ITY.

I still see Doggett in that red tuxedo,
introducing himself @ the opening
as Rasputin's father, the scene more
funeral than fete as the critic blogged:

*No art but for a mind/that boils therein./
A mind boils therein?* We fled ourselves
for a season, clutching our self-portraits,
we were ghosts long before we knew it.

Portrait of Us

1

I saw you through stained glass,
clipping dead wood from the birches.
I pulled my keys from my pocket,
& we were in Venice,
o labyrinthine city, labyrinthine heart,
a map that led to a secret piazza
where you fell to your knees in the rain.
I looked up from the photo album,
gutters were rusting on our roof,
the magnolia we planted had grown ten feet,
its white petals smoldering beneath a cloudless sky.
You splashed your face in the confession bowl,
& we followed our breath
beyond the office buildings with their fluorescent eyes,
into the woods between the apartments & the mall,
picked a basket of blackberries,
hedge thick with blackberries & crows,
a sliver of light before the wrecking ball smashed.
People say we rejoin the eternal body,
make a beeline homeward, but what good is this
without knowing, without memory?
Can life be said to exist
that can't reflect upon itself?

Heat sang in the leaves,
water murmured in the flowerpots.
You stretched across the bed, June panting
at the window, azalea blossoms pressed against glass.
Blue jays & golden finches splashed in the birdbath,
deer kept devouring the loose-leaf Hostas.
We nudged the clocks ahead & back,
holidays passed like a newsfeed.
One morning I saw three women
sitting on the stone bench beneath the red maple,

a man with a clipboard taking notes by the forsythia.
You whispered, *It's beginning again*,
& I thought, you can't divide
the multiple lives compressed to a single life,
the one life that tumbles into focus,
blurs & retreats into shadow,
the soundtrack of shifting templates,
that slow hemorrhaging of memory.
I searched the house, yelling your name,
rummaging inside myself, plundering
for wings, for an image or impulse
that might sling me toward empty frequencies.
I remembered the future, the end of the world,
what we'd get to witness, what we wouldn't.

Every room itches with your story,
days lost & sinking like a weighted body
into some cold, stygian trough—
so many faces irretrievable, voices irretrievable.
What color was the front door? Where was the mailbox?
What happened to the weathervane spinning above the chimney?
Markers so singular biodegrade, mulching
the amnesia from which a leafier knowing might emerge.
Or so I pray: & let love be my tether
even as I swallow an unchosen death,
that flash between knowing & deliverance.
What drives the blood to surge, a galaxy to rise & unravel,
that music never dies, the rest a kicking stillbirth.
Daily balms & burns remain my only gateway
into, out of other worlds, all part of this world,
which is no world at all,
the one world there is.

2

Mid-May I slammed my head on the doorframe,
a thin bell kept ringing in the wisteria.
Men with stethoscopes waited outside the van
as I examined a bottle cap on the sidewalk.
Did the suits need to keep their engine running?
Were drawn guns required?
Was the season so dire, the roots
of all held hallowed so at risk?
—returned in July as if not an hour had elapsed,
except that I read, friends say, like a different book.
Fragrances waft during descent that are hard
to bottle in a timeline, hard to play gumshoe
after the diagnosis. I said, *tending my love is
protecting the sacred from my own ambivalence.*
Did I reveal too much? Could someone point me
toward that laboratory where facts are concocted?

Evening arrives, my mother sobs
beneath the glowing dogwood,
my father paces on the patio,
stirring his martini with a ballpoint.
I keep treading these scenes,
a note floating in a red puddle,
a whistling in the driveway, the man in overalls
poised on a boulder beside the creek.
A blue light later, the cop filling out forms in the living room,
the minister's hand on my shoulder,
his wife's legs wrapped around my ribcage.

You asked, *What does faith have to do with libido?*
The motel curtains slid across the rod, a daytime
talk show blared in the honeymoon suite next-door.
You said, *give me the fire extinguisher.* You said,
but you didn't even know me then. I couldn't be sure.

I was a thousand men, you were a thousand women,
then too we were only one & one, & who knew what
avalanche was stirring. With me, it was all-in or fold;
cock & heart spoke one language, strived in tandem:
I never offered one organ, I didn't parcel myself out.
Did it strike you we were simply phenomena flirting
with gravity, colliding & colliding in the atmosphere?

The only salvation greater than love
is the possibility of love: the sky opens,
the gavel's hanging, all could be lost or gained,
a word from the ravishing stranger
erases reams of karma or forever snuffs the sun.
Deferment beats gratification every time
as long as the odds are in your favor.
Conversely ambivalence remains desire's source.
Lust recoils during a cease-fire,
ripens most heartily in a warzone.

Bodies are ticking bombs, & a pulsing vein
ran between us, a plea lodged in my throat,
not quite a salesman overturning a table,
more a magician who extracts semen
from the word *no*. I heard a theory once,
that God created the world as a distraction,
but this is no theory: passion that wears like a
tailored suit is nothing more than habit. Remember?
Over & over I came to you, each time as patient as an exile,
I unlaced your encryptions, traversed the code
frothing between us, & behold my empty pockets.

I talked to you through the night,
gripping a wire in the darkness
years after we hung up. You spoke of
torch singers & carnies, the usual ambassadors
emerging from unusual architecture.

In drier lands, you were the queen of the rain dance,
surfacing for the ritual from a series of oil mishaps.
The painting evolved after I turned a deeper shade of umber.
The portrait of us. But I knew a change was coming,
I saw the omens in the street, in the gallery,
in our living room: the vandal with the palette knife,
a rival from a previous venture,
insider versed on the composition of betrayal,
able to pop a lock or swing a safe with his eyes closed,
able to keep a steady hand during an earthquake.

I prayed for asylum.
I reached for you across the calendars,
you grabbed my arm, we pulled each other
into the closest heaven we could find,
back to the table, the easel, the negotiation.
We traveled so many circles of marrow,
our personal white light & brimstone,
though I can't recall each sprawling chapter,
page after page devoid of punctuation,
& then & then & then

3

The highway to you is lined
with boarded motels & the homeless of the world.
You're the petrol that feeds this primal engine,
cornfields near the border razed or smoking,
the Baptist billboards & machinery
abandoned in the aqueduct.
Fires erupt from behind police tape,
a few stragglers bellow epithets
before collapsing in the teargas.
I keep driving, as long as I keep driving.

I can't find you in the metropolitan night,
sprawl of excess, the ineluctable reminder
that millions were peeled from their psyches,
tongue-bound & mashed in a hull, then air thick with cotton,
then condominiums bloated with ivory gewgaws,
o globe charred & wheezing,
o America built by the black & poor.
I can't hear your voice for the sirens
blaring in the parking lot, the man with a bullhorn
touting a drug guaranteed to silence your incessant campaign.
Isn't that what every drug's for,
reprieve from a terror not quite your own?
—but no angel forgives its fall,
crashes a gate, crashes an airplane, pulls a trigger,
leaves a corpse in a tub or a ghost shrieking in a classroom.
I've learned from the nightmares of others,
my own are never that far,
clamoring at the table, fidgeting in the passenger seat.
I've learned to crack jokes,
my little Lucifers grin,
you could say we've become colleagues,
there's an understanding of sorts,
a thin rope stretching across the neutral zone.

                              How do I make the leap
                       from lying with my cock in my fist,
                           imagining you as more of
                              what you already are,
                                to claiming my place
                          on the left side of the savior?
              My teachers say love is the capacity to contain,
                          is evil the demand for release?
              I'm told that mastery's living at a threshold:
                                be the seed before
                           the root ruptures the husk,
                             emulate that moment
                           before the wave shatters,
                         before the first breath's given,
                         before the last breath's taken,
                                 before before

I creep through the dark mangroves,
feel you, hear you across the shallow bay
spitting salt water & kicking your feet.
Wind slides across the black surface,
ships are moored, sailors swap tales
in a bar that never closes, every story about you,
how you call to them, dragging them
across jagged rocks, dumping them on an island
where the pigs never sleep, how their fathers
& their grandfathers all knew you.
How many cruel tides have come & gone
since we first exchanged vows
along this pummeled coastline?
I can't make concessions. I prefer to be Crusoe
than hike inland after the sky's tantrum.
How often can I rearrange the wreckage in the sand?
Why spend another day bargaining with the dead?

Inside you,
I'm in another world,
deeper in this world,
where two worlds meet.
I wash up on a weedy shoal.
I look around for you,
gathering starfish & broken shells,
the gifts at my disposal,
resume the long stroking movement
through long brooding waters,
to finally fall in love with drowning,
to see it's possible
to love things
just as they are,
a woman
just as she is.

4

I hear the gangs hollering near the airport
as I circle the house where my mother,
wry Medea, forever mumbles to herself
in a room stale with doilies & potpourri,
one more Valium behind the curtain, her voice
swallowed & swallowed until it disappears.
I watch too my birth in the white room,
breath was a conversion, a virus annexing the flesh.
A hundred arms emerged from the shadows,
a hundred urgent hands waving in the glare,
each pressing a detail, a snapshot, tags embedded in my memory
like a chain buried in asphalt. The sky observed it all.
Later there was a dance, I can't recall the moves,
I signed a contract in a wide doorway with no one around.
It was the first time I betrayed myself,
dancing alone across an empty dancefloor.

A moment ago,
you were tending a potted amaryllis,
we were discussing a menu for Friday,
whether fish or chicken, beans or broccoli.
I yearn for the details once disdained,
a sugar pack under the leg of the dining-room table,
the Persian rug we moved an inch to the right,
lightbulbs that needed changing.
Heartbreak's the beauty
we're handed is already seizing:
I'm in love with what I call *you*,
but these illusions, so hypnotic,
have no place in the clouds.

I staggered down a stairwell,
you were in a garden across the wind,
I needed to alphabetize what was slipping from me,

slipped into ether, incomprehension, as I pressed
the last key of your number. The phone was ringing:
I was calling you, you stood in front of me,
perusing an x-ray. I was in a room that seemed
too quiet, you were repeating, *hello? hello?*
I careened through a familiar neighborhood, fumbling
our lingo, searching for an address in the rubble.
I thought it was noon, but all I could hear
were oily trumpets sputtering in the background.
I couldn't understand why so many comets
were flashing across the set at the wrong time.
I couldn't recognize the props I'd been given,
the machines & urgent voices, the pen
scratching across the clipboard, I couldn't
find my boats in the water, couldn't gauge the current
or nudge my intention toward a distant bank.
All I remember is how it destroyed me
to think no trace of our love could endure.

5

I say: *I grieve for everything beautiful*
    that arrives without reservation.
You reply: *look, the ivy's stalking the shingles.*
Then you're tugging a hose, watering the blue hydrangeas,
    fifty years clawing across my face.
Then ice on the leaves, ice on our mouths,
    ice in our lungs. I cry for the lovers we were,
    funnels we traveled, broad hallways
    that filtered into narrow rooms
filled with sunlight, greenery, & our favorite books.
    We walked as if we didn't know the earth
    would collapse beneath our steps,
    believing we were impervious to regret,
screamed into the treetops that we'd been forsaken.
    But the air expands & cramps,
    the waters mound & crumble,
    all flesh is home to the tyrant & the saint,
    how the story unfolds:
we dissolve into a moment, some eventual moment,
    what we resisted for countless lives,
    the birth & dispersion of light & matter,
    the word whose echo still stretches space.
Though all names are forgotten,
this remains: we uttered what the creator can't;
    the one music it needed from us,
    this is what we gave.

Acknowledgments

The author thanks the editors of the following journals, in which many of these poems first found a home:

Across the Margin, Hotel Amerika, Journal of Applied Poetics, Kentucky Review, Main Street Rag, Meat for Tea, Offcourse, Otoliths, Poetrybay, Random Sample, RHINO, Softblow, and *X-Peri.*

JOHN AMEN is the author of four previous collections of poetry: *Christening the Dancer*; *More of Me Disappears*; *At the Threshold of Alchemy*; and *strange theater*, finalist for the 2016 Brockman-Campbell Award. He is co-writer, along with Daniel Y. Harris, of *The New Arcana*. His work has been translated into Spanish, French, Hungarian, Korean, and Hebrew. In addition, he has released two folk/folk rock CDs: *All I'll Never Need* and *Ridiculous Empire*. He founded and continues to edit *The Pedestal Magazine*.

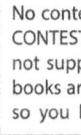

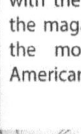

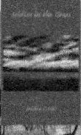

www.ingramcontent.com/pod-product-compliance
Lightning Source LLC
Chambersburg PA
CBHW022037090426
42741CB00007B/1094